SPORTS! SPORTS! SPORTS!

An I Can Read Book®

SPORTS! SPORTS! SPORTS!

A POETRY COLLECTION

Selected by LEE BENNETT HOPKINS
Pictures by BRIAN FLOCA

HarperTrophy®
An Imprint of HarperCollins*Publishers*

HarperCollins®, 📖®, Harper Trophy®, and I Can Read Book®
are trademarks of HarperCollins Publishers Inc.

Sports! Sports! Sports! *A Poetry Collection*
Copyright © 1999 by Lee Bennett Hopkins
Illustrations copyright © 1999 by Brian Floca
Printed in the U.S.A. All rights reserved.

Library of Congress Cataloging-in-Publication Data
Sports! sports! sports! : a poetry collection / selected by Lee Bennett Hopkins ;
pictures by Brian Floca.
   p.   cm. — (An I can read book)
   Summary: A collection of poems celebrating the joy and anguish of baseball, basketball,
football, ice hockey, soccer, skating, swimming, and running races.
   ISBN 0-06-027800-5. — ISBN 0-06-027801-3 (lib. bdg.) — ISBN 0-06-443713-2 (pbk.)
   1. Sports—Juvenile poetry.   2. Children's poetry, American.   [1. Sports—Poetry.
2. American poetry—Collections.]   I. Hopkins, Lee Bennett.   II. Floca, Brian, ill.
III. Series.
PS595.S78S66   1999   98-8509
811'.54080355—DC21   CIP
                                                                  AC

❖

First Harper Trophy edition, 2000

Visit us on the World Wide Web!
www.harperchildrens.com

ACKNOWLEDGMENTS

Thanks are due to the following for permission to reprint the works listed below:

Curtis Brown, Ltd., for "Hoop Dreams" and "Outfielder" by Rebecca Kai Dotlich. Copyright © 1999 by Rebecca Kai Dotlich; "Any Excuse Will Do" and "Fast Track" by Nikki Grimes. Copyright © 1999 by Nikki Grimes; "High Dive" and "Night Game" by Lee Bennett Hopkins. Copyright © 1999 by Lee Bennett Hopkins. All reprinted by permission of Curtis Brown, Ltd.

Sandra Gilbert Brüg for "Soccer Feet." Used by permission of the author, who controls all rights.

Lillian M. Fisher for "I'm Running" and "Play Ball." Used by permission of the author, who controls all rights.

Lee Bennett Hopkins for "Hero" by Tom Robert Shields. Used by permission of Lee Bennett Hopkins for the author.

Kate Hovey for "Patch Lesson." Used by permission of the author, who controls all rights.

Tony Johnston for "After the Game." Used by permission of the author, who controls all rights.

J. Patrick Lewis for "A Football Poem." Used by permission of the author, who controls all rights.

Carl Pech for "Fly Balls." Used by permission of the author, who controls all rights.

Marian Reiner for "Ice Skating" by Sandra Liatsos. Copyright © 1999 by Sandra Liatsos; "O Beautiful Here" from *A Crazy Flight and Other Poems* by Myra Cohn Livingston. Copyright © 1969; copyright © renewed 1997 by Myra Cohn Livingston. All reprinted by permission of Marian Reiner for the authors.

Lawrence Schimel for "Basketball Dreams," "Ice Hockey," and "Running Out of Breath." Used by permission of the author, who controls all rights.

Michael R. Strickland for "Guess What!" Used by permission of the author, who controls all rights.

ALSO BY LEE BENNETT HOPKINS

I CAN READ BOOKS®

Blast Off! Poems About Space
More Surprises
Questions
Surprises
Weather

PICTURE BOOKS

Best Friends
By Myself
Good Books, Good Times!
Good Rhymes, Good Times
Morning, Noon and Nighttime, Too
The Sky Is Full of Song

BOOKS FOR MIDDLE GRADE

Click, Rumble, Roar
Mama and Her Boys

PROFESSIONAL READING

Let Them Be Themselves
Pass the Poetry, Please!
Pauses: Autobiographical Reflections of
101 Creators of Children's Books

To my great-nephew—
Joseph Edward Yavorski
—L.B.H.

For my grandmother,
Dorris Floca
—B.F.

FLY BALLS

by Carl Pech

I am like a spider,

So it's fly balls that I love.

For I catch them

  when they're buzzing,

In the webbing of my glove.

OUTFIELDER

by Rebecca Kai Dotlich

Batter's up.

Not a sound.

Knees bent.

Glove to ground.

Face to crowd.

Back to sun.

Hoping to stop

just *one* home run.

PLAY BALL!

by Lillian M. Fisher

It was my turn to bat

And I hit the ball

So hard it sailed

Right over the wall.

The crowd went wild.

I started to run.

How happy I'd be

If my team won.

First base, second,

third—I'm home free!

Hurrah for my team!

Hurrah for *me*!

FAST TRACK

by Nikki Grimes

When the whistle blows

I am ready and set

and no one can tell me

I am too anything

or less than enough.

I am a tornado of legs and feet

and warm wind whipping past

everyone else on the track

and all that's on my mind

is scissoring through

the finish line.

I'M RUNNING

by Lillian M. Fisher

I'm running, I'm running

With wind in my face

And wings on my heels

To win first place

Or maybe second

Even third if I try

'Cause everyone's running

Faster than I.

But I'll keep on going

And take it in stride

If I lose—so what?

At least I tried!

RUNNING OUT OF BREATH

by Lawrence Schimel

Round and round
The endless track—
We run but keep
Circling back

To where we were
Once before.
I run one lap,
Then two, three, four.

I'm out of breath

But see me smile

I'm so proud—

I ran a mile!

HIGH DIVE

by Lee Bennett Hopkins

I leap.

I lunge.

I plunge headfirst.

Sailing, soaring, falling

I go

d

o

w

n

into the

blue

below.

O BEAUTIFUL HERE

by *Myra Cohn Livingston*

O beautiful here, water

Bubbles in clear foam,

Warming to the sun at top,

Shivery to the bone:

Floating in cool nothingness

Blue pool waters brim:

O beautiful here, water,

Weightless, I swim.

GUESS WHAT!

by Michael R. Strickland

Black and white

Kicked with might

Smooth and round

Air bound

Passed and rolled

Toward the goal

Rise and fall

A soccer ball.

SOCCER FEET

by Sandra Gilbert Brüg

Soccer player's nimble feet

hustle at the soccer meet

    Kick it   move it

    zig zag   slide

Clad in cleats they spin and glide

    Steal it   hop it

    pass it   pop it

Toward the net. Who can stop it?

Dribble dribble faster more

SLAM that checkered ball

to SCORE!

ANY EXCUSE WILL DO

by Nikki Grimes

Summer basketball—

drops of sweat blur my sight. I

can't quite see the hoop.

HOOP DREAM

by Rebecca Kai Dotlich

The sound of the ball

as it drums the ground.

The fans in the stands

who are held spellbound.

The tick of the clock.

The feel of the floor.

One quick, sure step,

then shoot to score!

BASKETBALL DREAMS

by Lawrence Schimel

Dribble, dribble

to the right.

Cross the court.

Score is tight.

Can my steady

hand and eye

sink the basket?

End the tie?

AFTER THE GAME

by Tony Johnston

The game is over.

But the gym still

thrums

with the basketball's

THUMP—

       THUMP—

              THUMPY

hum.

HERO

by Tom Robert Shields

October comes with

Chill air—

Golden sun—

A football game—

A score of

Six to zero—

And my brother runs

A winning touchdown

And becomes

My instant hero.

A FOOTBALL POEM

by J. Patrick Lewis

A football poem

Should hit hard

Like a nose guard,

Or sail the sky

Like a long pass

On *real* grass.

A football poem

Should score

Inside the five

On fourth and four.

A football poem

Should sweat and grunt . . .

Or punt.

ICE-SKATING

by *Sandra Liatsos*

Come and glide

across the pond.

We'll soar and sing

a flying song.

Beneath our skates

the clouds will fly

and sun will light

the icy sky.

PATCH LESSON

by Kate Hovey

The silver blade

Of one white skate

Cuts a perfect figure 8.

42

A single line

Of pure, precise

Poetry inscribed on ice.

ICE HOCKEY

by Lawrence Schimel

My skates go skidding

cross the ice.

I go spinning

once, twice.

My hockey stick

hits the puck.

I score a goal!

Part skill, part luck.

NIGHT GAME

by *Lee Bennett Hopkins*

I'm a winner.

    A *winner*.

I never, ever lose

At any sport or game I play—

At anything I choose.

I'm a winner.

The *best* on any team.

When I'm alone

In bed at night

and dream . . .

and dream . . .

and dream.

INDEX OF AUTHORS AND TITLES

After the Game, 35

Any Excuse Will Do, 28

Basketball Dreams, 32

Brüg, Sandra Gilbert, 26

Dotlich, Rebecca Kai,
   10, 31

Fast Track, 15

Fisher, Lillian M., 12, 16

Fly Balls, 9

Football Poem, A, 38

Grimes, Nikki, 15, 28

Guess What!, 24

Hero, 36

High Dive, 20

Hoop Dream, 31,

Hopkins, Lee Bennett,
   20, 46

Hovey, Kate, 42

Ice Hockey, 44

Ice-Skating, 41

I'm Running, 16

Johnston, Tony, 35

Lewis, J. Patrick, 38

Liatsos, Sandra, 41

Livingston, Myra Cohn, 23

Night Game, 46

O Beautiful Here, 23

Outfielder, 10

Patch Lesson, 42

Pech, Carl, 9

Play Ball!, 12

Running Out of Breath, 18

Schimel, Lawrence,
   18, 32, 44

Shields, Tom Robert, 36

Soccer Feet, 26

Strickland, Michael R., 24